The Turtle Dove's Journey

A STORY OF MIGRATION

MADELEINE DUNPHY   Illustrated by **MARLO GARNSWORTHY**

Web of Life

CHILDREN'S BOOKS

For my Thursday Night Group, with so much love and appreciation. —M.D.

To Jonquil: fly free, fly far, sweetheart. —M.G.

Special thanks to Dr. John Mallord, Chris Orsman, and Nigel Butcher
of the Royal Society for the Protection of Birds for their invaluable scientific
expertise and for their dedication to the protection of turtle doves.

For information, write to:
Web of Life Children's Books
P.O. Box 2726, Berkeley, California 94702
www.weboflifebooks.com

Published in the United States in 2020 by Web of Life Children's Books.
Printed in China

Library of Congress Control Number: 2019942546
ISBN 978-1-970039-01-6

The artwork for this book was prepared using watercolor collage and digital oil.

For more information about our books and the authors and artists who create them,
visit our website: www.weboflifebooks.com

Distributed by Publishers Group West/An Ingram Brand
(800)788-3123 · www.pgw.com

Production Date: 5-22-19
Plant & Location: Printed in Guangdong, China
Job / Batch # 84453/EPC 903026

FSC
www.fsc.org
MIX
Paper from
responsible sources
FSC® C124385

SOUTH AMER

NORTH AMERICA

EUROPE

AFRICA

Suffolk, England, 4–5

London, England, 6–7

English Channel, 8–9

Bordeaux, France, 10–11

Madrid, Spain, 12–13

Seville, Spain, 14–15

Strait of Gibraltar, 16–17

Casablanca, Morocco, 18–19

Atlas Mountains, 20–21

This book is about
a turtle dove's
migration from
England to Mali.
The labels on this
map show the places
the dove visits along
the way, and the
numbers indicate
the corresponding
pages in the book.

Western Sahara, 22–23

Mauritania, 24–25

Foret de Bandia Reserve,
Senegal, 26–27

Mali, 28–31

The turtle dove perches in a garden in Suffolk, England. This is where he and his mate raised their chicks. It is now September, and with every passing day the weather is cooler and there is less and less sunlight. Hopping from branch to branch, the turtle dove is restless. Something inside is telling him it is time to fly away.

He waits until night and then starts his migration south. He will travel all the way from England to Mali—a distance of more than 4,000 miles (6,400 km). It will take him about a month to travel this far.

You might wonder how the turtle dove knows where he is going. The answer is instinct: He was born knowing where to fly. He also uses the rising and setting sun as his compass. And he remembers sights and smells from previous migrations that can help him to know where he is. In the distance, he recognizes a familiar twinkle

When migrating, the turtle dove flies at night because it is safer. If he traveled during the day, predators like falcons and hawks could easily see him. But at nighttime, these predators are asleep.

Tonight, the turtle dove flies over the English Channel, a body of water separating England and France. Traveling at a speed of 37 miles (60 km) an hour, the turtle dove moves faster than the ships sailing below. He reaches the north coast of France and continues south to...

…Bordeaux, where a great expanse of vineyards is bathed in the light of the rising sun.

While migrating, the dove eats and sleeps during the day. This morning, he finds a Juneberry hedge, nestles deep inside, and falls asleep. He is so well camouflaged that even a peregrine falcon overhead cannot see him.

Tonight, the turtle dove travels over Madrid, Spain. Heavy rain pounds against the bird's body, making flying tiring. Even though he usually flies through the night, the dove slowly descends and lands under the eaves of an ornate building to rest.

A gargoyle on the ledge above looks down on him while he preens his wet feathers. He perches here until the rain lets up and then travels to…

...Seville for a few days of resting and eating. He has already flown more than 1,400 miles (over 2,200 km) on his journey. While in Seville, he encounters other turtle doves, who are also migrating south.

They gather at a farm on the outskirts of the city, where they peacefully peck at the ground, eating wheat and sunflower seeds. The birds are saving their strength and refueling their bodies, for tonight they will travel to Africa...

…over the Strait of Gibraltar. This is the shortest link between Europe and Africa, so millions of migratory birds who don't like traveling over water take this route each year. The turtle dove is joined by whitethroats and blackcaps, willow warblers and chiffchaffs.

In the distance, the spectacular Rock of Gibraltar juts from the sea. Clouds of birds swirl above the high cliffs, their dark shapes visible against the full moon.

Another benefit of flying at night is that the dove is less likely to get dehydrated from the high temperatures and the heat of the sun. But tonight, he is thirsty. He flies low, keeping a lookout for water, and spies a burbling fountain by a mosque in Casablanca, Morocco. He guzzles down several beakfuls and then continues south to...

...the Atlas Mountains, a series of mountain ranges stretching more than 1,200 miles (about 1,900 km) through northwestern Africa. The wind blows down the canyons like water flows down a river.

Strong winds can be good or bad for the dove. If they are moving in the wrong direction, they can push him off course. But if they are heading in the right direction, they can help him fly with much less effort. Tonight, the winds carry him south until he is flying...

...over the Sahara, the largest desert in the world. This is the most dangerous part of his journey. Water and shade are scarce here, and sandstorms can occur. Tonight, blustering winds pull sand, dirt, and pebbles from the ground and blast them into the sky. Sandstorms can reach heights of 1 mile (1.6 km) or even higher. Luckily, this storm is relatively mild, and the turtle dove flies above it—much like an airplane can fly above a rainstorm.

Four days later...

...the turtle dove arrives exhausted in Mauritania. He stops at an oasis—a lush green area where water can be found, surrounded by desert. Although the sun is blazing, he finds shelter under a cliff's ledge, where it is shady. He falls asleep to the rustle of palm fronds and the slurping of camels. He no longer needs to fly as far each night because he is nearing the end of his journey.

A few days late r, he continues south to a nature reserve in...

...Senegal, where hundreds of other turtle doves are drinking and bathing at a riverbank. Small groups of doves take turns at the water's edge or in the shallows. They gulp down water quickly and then flee to the treetops to avoid predators, like the jackal, who might be lurking.

Some of these birds will stay here for the winter, while others will continue on. The turtle dove spends a couple of days here and then travels eastward...

...to Mali, where he meets a flock of over a thousand turtle doves! The faint whistle of their flapping wings fills the air.

He skims over fields of rice, millet, and sorghum, where he pauses for an afternoon snack. A nearby river provides a refreshing drink and bath. The turtle dove then flies high and drops steeply toward some acacia trees—a safe place to sleep.

Everything he needs is here

Night is approaching, and the turtle dove joins the flock among the acacias. The birds jostle about, fluttering their wings, calling to each other softly. Once it is dark, the doves fall silent. This is the end of his journey, and the turtle dove can finally sleep at night.

It has been four weeks since he left England. During his migration, he braved sandstorms, flew over seas, and navigated windswept mountains, mostly in darkness. Next April, he will make the long journey to England to raise another family.

But for now, he is home.

MORE ABOUT TURTLE DOVES

The Turtle Dove's Journey is based on the migration of a real turtle dove that was tracked with satellite telemetry by the Royal Society for the Protection of Birds (RSPB). Turtle doves spend about a third of the year in Europe, where they breed and raise young. Sometime in August or September, they leave their breeding grounds and start their migration south through western Europe to the warmer climate of sub-Saharan West Africa. They spend about six months in Africa before returning to Europe in April.

The turtle dove is the only long-distance migratory dove species in Europe. Plentiful food in Africa during the European winter and better nesting sites in Europe during the summer are thought to be the main reasons for turtle dove migration. No one really knows why turtle doves migrate, while similar dove species remain in Europe or Africa all year long.

While many turtle dove pairs are lifelong mates, some mate for only one breeding season and stay together only until their chicks are grown. The chicks are usually the first of the family to leave on migration. After the chicks have left, the males are usually next to depart.

The bird in this book is a European turtle dove of the subspecies *Streptopelia turtur turtur*. There are three other subspecies of turtle doves.

RSPB started tracking European turtle doves on their migrations to gain information about why this bird's population has declined so severely. Studies show that the European turtle dove's population has decreased by 78% since 1980, and in England, where the bird in this book originates, this species' population has decreased by 93% since 1994. Because of this, the turtle dove is listed as a vulnerable species in the International Union for Conservation of Nature Red List of Threatened Species.

There are several reasons for this dramatic decline. Changes in agricultural practices are thought to be the main culprit. There are more farms and fewer natural habitats than in the past. Because of this, the turtle dove's diet is now dependent on human-grown crops. While these crops provide sustenance to the dove, they are not as healthy as the dove's natural diet of seeds from wild plants. Another problem is the removal of the hedgerows and scrub where turtle doves used to nest. Doves are forced to choose less suitable nesting sites, making them more visible and vulnerable to predators. Hunting—both legal and illegal—is also a serious risk to the doves as they migrate through France, Spain, Morocco, and Senegal. Finally, drought and disease have also decreased the turtle doves' population.

We must do what we can to help protect the turtle dove and other bird species from extinction. Please contact the organizations listed below to find out what you can do to help ensure the survival of this magnificent bird.

Royal Society for the Protection of Birds
www.rspb.org.uk

Operation Turtle Dove
www.operationturtledove.org

BirdLife International
www.birdlife.org